Communities of Salt and Light
Reflections on the
Social Mission of the Parish

UNITED STATES CONFERENCE OF CATHOLIC BISHOPS
WASHINGTON, D.C.

Communities of Salt and Light: Reflections on the Social Mission of the Parish was developed by two conference committees: Domestic Social Policy and International Policy. After review and approval by both committees, the statement was approved by the Administrative Board in September 1993 and by the Catholic bishops of the United States at their General Meeting in November 1993. *Communities of Salt and Light: Reflections on the Social Mission of the Parish* is authorized for publication as a statement of the National Conference of Catholic Bishops by the undersigned.

Monsignor Robert N. Lynch
General Secretary, NCCB/USCC

ISBN: 978-1-57455-764-0

First printing, Revised Edition, July 2006
Fourth printing, Revised Edition, June 2013

In 2001 the National Conference of Catholic Bishops (NCCB) and the United States Catholic Conference (USCC) became the United States Conference of Catholic Bishops (USCCB).

Cover graphic by Rabil and Associates, Gaithersburg, Maryland.

Text graphics copyright © 1992, Catholic News Service, Washington, DC. Used with permission. All rights reserved.

Scripture texts used in this work are taken from the *New American Bible*, copyright © 1991, 1986, and 1970 by the Confraternity of Christian Doctrine, Washington, DC 20017, and are used by permission of the copyright owner. All rights reserved.

Contents

Introductory Note: These reflections offer a basic resource for pastors, parish leaders, and parishioners seeking to strengthen the social ministry of their parish. This bishops' reflection represents neither major new teaching nor a new national program. Rather, it brings together the principles of our social teaching and local pastoral experience in an overall orientation and general framework for parish social ministry. This statement is complemented by a companion video and a resource guide (also available from USCCB Publishing) designed to help parishes assess and explore in practical ways the social mission of their own parish.

Introduction

The parish is where the Church lives. Parishes are communities of faith, of action, and of hope. They are where the gospel is proclaimed and celebrated, where believers are formed and sent to renew the earth. Parishes are the home of the Christian community; they are the heart of our Church. Parishes are the place where God's people meet Jesus in word and sacrament and come in touch with the source of the Church's life.

One of the most encouraging signs of the gospel at work in our midst is the vitality and quality of social justice ministries in our parishes. Across the country, countless local communities of faith are serving those in need, working for justice, and sharing our social teaching as never before. Millions of parishioners are applying the gospel and church teaching in their own families, work, and communities. More and more, the social justice dimensions of our faith are moving from the fringes of parishes to become an integral part of local Catholic life.

We welcome and applaud this growing recognition of and action on the social mission of the parish. We offer these brief reflections to affirm and support pastors and parish leaders in this essential task and to encourage all parishes to take up this challenge with renewed commitment, creativity, and urgency.

In the past decade, we have written major pastoral letters on peace and economic justice and issued pastoral statements on a number of important issues touching human life and human dignity. But until now, we have not specifically addressed the crucial role of parishes in the Church's social ministry. We offer these words of support, encouragement, and challenge at this time because we are convinced that the local parish is the most important ecclesial setting for sharing and acting on our Catholic social heritage. We hope that these reflections can help pastors, parish staffs, parish councils, social concerns committees, and other parishioners strengthen the social justice dimensions of their own parish life. This focus on the social mission of the parish complements and strengthens the call to evangelization found in our statement *Go and Make Disciples: A National Plan and Strategy for Catholic Evangelization in the United States.*

We offer a framework for integration rather than a specific model or new national program. We seek to affirm and encourage local parish commitment and creativity in social ministry. We know pastors and parish leaders do not need another program to carry forward or more expectations to meet. We see the parish dimensions of social ministry not as an added burden, but as a part of what keeps a parish alive and makes it truly Catholic. Effective social ministry helps the parish not only do more, but be more—more of a reflection of the gospel, more of a worshiping and evangelizing people, more of a faithful community. It is an essential part of parish life.

This is not a new message, but it takes on new urgency in light of the increasing clarity and strength of Catholic social teaching and the signs of declining respect for human life and human dignity in society. We preach a gospel of justice and peace in a rapidly changing world and troubled nation. Our faith is tested by the violence, injustice, and moral confusion that surround us. In this relatively affluent nation, a fourth of our children under six grow up in poverty.[1] Each year in our nation, 1.6 million children are destroyed before birth by abortion.[2] And every day, 40,000 children die from hunger and its consequences around the world.[3] In our streets and neighborhoods, violence destroys the hopes, dreams, and lives of too many children. In our local communities, too many cannot find decent work, housing, health care, or education. In our families, parents struggle to raise children with dignity, hope, and basic values.

The pursuit of justice and peace is an essential part of what makes a parish Catholic.

Our faith stands in marked contrast to these grim realities. At a time of rampant individualism, we stand for family and community. At a time of intense consumerism, we insist it is not what we have, but how we treat one another that counts. In an age that does not value permanence or hard work in relationships, we believe marriage is forever and children are a blessing, not a burden. At a time of growing isolation, we remind our nation of its responsibility to the broader world, to pursue peace, to welcome immigrants, to protect the lives of hurting children and refugees. At a time when the rich are getting richer and the poor are getting poorer, we insist the moral test of our society is how we treat and care for the weakest among us.

In these challenging days, we believe that the Catholic community needs to be more than ever a source of clear moral vision and effective action. We are called to be the "salt of the earth" and "light of the world" in the words of the Scriptures (cf. Mt 5:13-16). This task belongs to every believer and every parish. It cannot be assigned to a few or simply delegated to diocesan or national structures. The pursuit of justice and peace is an essential part of what makes a parish Catholic.

In urban neighborhoods, in suburban communities, and in rural areas, parishes serve as anchors of hope and communities of caring, help families meet their own needs and reach out to others, and serve as centers of community life and networks of assistance.

The Roots of
Parish Social Mission

The roots of this call to justice and charity are in the Scriptures, especially in the Hebrew prophets and the life and words of Jesus. Parish social ministry has clear biblical roots.

In the gospel according to Luke, Jesus began his public life by reading a passage from Isaiah that introduced his ministry and the mission of every parish. The parish must proclaim the transcendent message of the gospel and help:

- ← bring "good news to the poor" in a society where millions lack the necessities of life;
- ← bring "liberty to captives" when so many are enslaved by poverty, addiction, ignorance, discrimination, violence, or disabling conditions;
- ← bring "new sight to the blind" in a culture where the excessive pursuit of power or pleasure can spiritually blind us to the dignity and rights of others; and
- ← "set the downtrodden free" in communities where crime, racism, family disintegration, and economic and moral forces leave people without real hope (cf. Lk 4:18).

Our parish communities are measured by how they serve "the least of these" in our parish and beyond its boundaries—the hungry, the homeless, the sick, those in prison, the stranger (cf. Mt 25:31). Our local families of faith are called to "hunger and thirst for justice" and to be "peacemakers" in our own communities (cf. Mt 5:6, 9). A parish cannot really proclaim the gospel if its message is not reflected in its own community life. The biblical call to charity, justice, and peace claims not only each believer, but also each community where believers gather for worship, formation, and pastoral care.

Over the last century, these biblical mandates have been explored and expressed in a special way in Catholic social teaching. The central message is simple: our faith is profoundly social. We cannot be called truly "Catholic" unless we hear and heed the Church's call to serve those in need and work for justice and peace. We cannot call ourselves followers of Jesus unless we take up his mission of bringing "good news to the poor, liberty to captives, and new sight to the blind" (cf. Lk 4:18).

The Church teaches that social justice is an integral part of evangelization, a constitutive dimension of preaching the gospel, and an essential part of the Church's mission. The links between justice and evangelization are strong and vital. We cannot proclaim a gospel we do not live, and we cannot carry out a real social ministry without knowing the Lord and hearing his call to justice and peace. Parish communities must show by their deeds of love and justice that the gospel they proclaim is fulfilled in their actions. This tradition is not empty theory; it challenges our priorities as a nation, our choices as a Church, our values as parishes. It has led the Church to stand with the poor and vulnerable against the strong and powerful. It brings occasional controversy and conflict, but it also brings life and vitality to the People of God. It is a sign of our faithfulness to the gospel.

The center of the Church's social teaching is the life, dignity, and rights of the human person. We are called in a special way to serve the poor and vulnerable; to build bridges of solidarity among peoples of differing races and nations, language and ability, gender and culture. Family life and work have special places in Catholic social teaching; the rights of the unborn, families, workers, immigrants, and the poor deserve special protection. Our tradition also calls us to show our respect for the Creator by our care for creation and our commitment to work for environmental justice. This vital tradition is an essential resource for parish life. It offers a framework and direction for our social ministry, calling us to concrete works of charity, justice, and peacemaking.[4]

The Social Mission of the Parish: A Framework of Integration

I n responding to the Scriptures and the principles of Catholic, social teaching, parishes are not called to an extra or added dimension of our faith,
but to a central demand of Catholic life and evangelization. We recognize
the sometimes overwhelming demands on parish leadership and resources. We
know it is easier to write about these challenges than to carry them out day
by day. But we believe the Church's social mission is an essential measure
of every parish community, and it needs more attention and support within
our parishes.

Our parishes are enormously diverse—in where and who they serve,
in structures and resources, in their members and leaders. This diversity is
reflected in how parishes shape their social ministry. The depth and range of
activity are most impressive. Across our country, parishioners offer their time,
their money, and their leadership to a wide variety of efforts to meet needs
and change structures. Parishes
are deeply involved in meeting
their members' needs, serving the
hungry and homeless, welcoming the stranger and immigrant,
reaching out to troubled families,
advocating for just public policies,
organizing for safer and better
communities, and working creatively for a more peaceful world. Our communities and ministries have been greatly enriched and nourished by the faith
and wisdom of parishioners who experience injustice and all those who work
for greater justice.

*We believe the Church's
social mission is an
essential measure of every
parish community.*

There has been tremendous growth of education, outreach, advocacy,
and organizing in parishes. From homeless shelters to prayer services, from
food pantries to legislative networks, from global education programs to neighborhood organizing, parishes are responding. But in some parishes the social

P arishioners at St. John the Baptist in Silver Spring, Maryland, try to reflect their concern for the poor during each Sunday liturgy. Parishioners bring donations of food to Mass which are included in the Offertory and later distributed through a food pantry. Regular preaching on the gospel's call for justice and peace, as well as consistent prayers for those in need during the General Intercessions, help St. John's parish community connect its social mission with worship.

justice dimensions of parish life are still neglected, underdeveloped, or touch only a few parishioners.

We have much to learn from those parishes that are leading the way in making social ministry an integral part of parish ministry and evangelization. We need to build local communities of faith where our social teaching is central, not fringe; where social ministry is integral, not optional; where it is the work of every believer, not just the mission of a few committed people and committees.

For too many parishioners, our social teaching is an unknown tradition. In too many parishes, social ministry is a task for a few, not a challenge for the entire parish community. We believe we are just beginning to realize our potential as a community of faith committed to serve those in need and to work for greater justice.

The parishes that are leaders in this area see social ministry not as a specialized ministry, but as an integral part of the entire parish. They weave the Catholic social mission into every aspect of parish life—worship, formation, and action. They follow a strategy of integration and collaboration, which keeps social ministry from becoming isolated or neglected.

A framework of integration might include the following elements.

Anchoring Social Ministry: Prayer and Worship

The most important setting for the Church's social teaching is not in a food pantry or in a legislative committee room, but in prayer and worship, especially

The consistent life ethic is the theme around which social ministry is organized at St. Isaac Jogues Parish in Orlando, Florida. The parish respect life coordinator works with other parish leaders on activities and advocacy in such areas as pro-life, aging, disabilities, and social justice. Together, they try to root their work in prayer and in the common theme of the dignity of human life. In November, they sponsor a Consistent Life Ethic Prayer Service, to which they invite members of the parish and members of other nearby churches. In January, they sponsor a prayer service that focuses on nonviolence—before and after birth. On St. Francis Day, they sponsor a blessing of animals.

"We hope these events are opportunities for conversion," says parishioner Deborah Shearer. "In addition to times of prayer, they are opportunities for education on the full meaning of respect for life."

gathered around the altar for the eucharist. It is in the liturgy that we find the fundamental direction, motivation, and strength for social ministry. Social ministry not genuinely rooted in prayer can easily burn itself out. On the other hand, worship that does not reflect the Lord's call to conversion, service, and justice can become pious ritual and empty of the gospel.

We support new efforts to integrate liturgy and justice, to make clear that we are one people united in faith, worship, and works of charity and justice. We need to be a Church that helps believers recognize Jesus in the breaking of the bread and those without bread. Eucharist, penance, confirmation, and the other sacraments have essential social dimensions that ought to be appropriately reflected in how we celebrate, preach, and pray. Those who plan and preside at our worship can help the parish community understand more clearly the spiritual and scriptural roots of our pursuit of justice without distorting or imposing on the liturgy.

Our social ministry must be anchored in prayer, where we uncover the depths of God's call to seek justice and pursue peace. In personal prayer, the reading of the Scriptures, and quiet reflection on the Christian vocation, we discover the social mission of every believer. In serving those in need, we serve the Lord. In seeking justice and peace, we witness to the reign of God in our midst. In prayer, we find the reasons, the strength, and the call to follow Jesus in the ways of charity, justice, and peace.

Sharing the Message:
Preaching and Education

We are called to share our social teaching more effectively in our parishes than we have. Our social doctrine is an integral part of our faith; we need to pass it on clearly, creatively, and consistently. It is a remarkable spiritual, intellectual, and pastoral resource that has been too little known or appreciated even in our own community.

Preaching that reflects the social dimensions of the gospel is indispensable. Priests should not and need not impose an agenda on the liturgy to preach about justice. Rather, we urge those who preach not to ignore the regular opportunities provided by the liturgy to connect our faith and our everyday lives, to share biblical values on justice and peace. Week after week, day after day, the lectionary calls the community to reflect on the scriptural message of justice and peace. The pulpit is not a partisan rostrum and to try to make it one would be a mistake, but preaching that ignores the social dimensions of our faith does not truly reflect the gospel of Jesus Christ.

Our social doctrine must also be an essential part of the curriculum and life of our schools, religious education programs, sacramental preparation,

Young people learn firsthand about the social mission of the Church at St. Mary's Parish in Richmond, Virginia. Beginning in junior high school, every religious education class selects a single social issue on which to focus both direct service and advocacy during the school year. Last year the class, whose issue was homelessness, served food at a homeless shelter and assisted with a parish-sponsored sheltering program. They also wrote to their state legislators encouraging increased funding for homeless programs and a state Earned Income Tax Credit (EITC) to help the working poor.

and Christian initiation activities. We need to share and celebrate our common social heritage as Catholics, developing materials and training tools that ensure that we are sharing our social teaching in every educational ministry of our parishes. Every parish should regularly assess how well our social teaching is shared in its formation and educational ministries.

Supporting the "Salt of the Earth": Family, Work, Citizenship

Our parishes are clearly called to help people live their faith in the world, helping them to understand and act on the social dimensions of the gospel in their everyday lives. National statements, diocesan structures, or parish committees can be useful, but they are no substitute for the everyday choices and commitments of believers—acting as parents, workers, students, owners, investors, advocates, policy makers and citizens.

For example, parishes are called to support their members in:

← building and sustaining marriages of quality, fidelity, equality, and permanence in an age that does not value commitment or hard work in relationships;

← raising families with gospel values in a culture where materialism, selfishness, and prejudice still shape so much of our lives;

← being a good neighbor; welcoming newcomers and immigrants; treating people of different races, ethnic groups, and nationalities with respect and kindness;

← seeing themselves as evangelizers who recognize the unbreakable link between spreading the gospel and work for social justice;

← bringing Christian values and virtues into the marketplace;

← treating co-workers, customers, and competitors with respect and fairness, demonstrating economic initiative, and practicing justice;

← bringing integrity and excellence to public service and community responsibilities, seeking the common good, respecting human life, and promoting human dignity;

← providing leadership in unions, community groups, professional associations, and political organizations at a time of rising cynicism and indifference.

In short, our parishes need to encourage, support, and sustain lay people in living their faith in the family, neighborhood, marketplace, and public arena. It is lay women and men, placing their gifts at the service of others (cf. 1 Pt 4:10), who will be God's primary instruments in renewing the earth by their leadership and faithfulness in the community. The most challenging work for justice is not done in church committees, but in the secular world of work, family life, and citizenship.

"In this situation, what does love—the commitment to others and the needy among us—require?" This kind of question might be posed by one of eighteen Vocation Reflection Groups sponsored by St. Martha's Parish in Akron, Ohio. Open to all in the community, the groups are organized by occupation—lawyers, educators, counsellors, journalists, and others—as well as one general group for those who do not fit in the other seventeen. They meet monthly to reflect on their work and to discuss how they can apply their beliefs and values in their workplaces. Fr. Norman Douglas, pastor of St. Martha's, helps lay facilitators from each group plan each meeting. Occasional workshops and panels provide in-service educational credits.

During Sunday liturgies, Fr. Douglas also tries to acknowledge how people's work life is related to ministry. For example, when the readings focus on Jesus as healer, those involved in health care occupations are invited to stand after communion for a special blessing. "We try to infuse the spirituality of all of life into what is already going on in the parish," explains Fr. Douglas. "We focus on practical spirituality lived out in the real world."

Serving the "Least of These": Outreach and Charity

Parishes are called to reach out to the hurting, the poor, and the vulnerable in our midst in concrete acts of charity. Just as the gospel tells us our lives will be judged by our response to the "least of these," so too our parishes should be measured by our help for the hungry, the homeless, the troubled, and the alienated—in our own community and beyond. This is an area of creativity and initiative with a wide array of programs, partnerships with Catholic Charities, and common effort with other churches. Thousands of food pantries; hundreds of shelters; and uncounted outreach programs for poor families, refugees, the elderly, and others in need are an integral part of parish life. The parish is the most significant place where new immigrants and refugees are welcomed into our Church and community. A Church that teaches an option for the poor must reflect that option in our service of those in need. Parish efforts to meet human needs also provide valuable experience, expertise, and credibility in advocating for public policy to address the forces that leave people in need of our charity.

Catholic teaching calls us to serve those in need and to change the structures that deny people their dignity and rights as children of God. Service and action, charity and justice are complementary components of parish social ministry. Neither alone is sufficient; both are essential signs of the gospel at work. A parish serious about social ministry will offer opportunities to serve those in need and to advocate for justice and peace. These are not competing priorities, but two dimensions of the same fundamental mission to protect the life and dignity of the human person.

St. Augustine's Parish in Spokane, Washington, combines service to those in need in the local community with international outreach. When Catholic Charities purchased the former Shriners Hospital, the parish social concerns committee mobilized volunteers to sort through the beds, wheelchairs, and other medical equipment that it contained and ship it to West Africa for use in a children's hospital in Ghana. What was not shipped was auctioned, with proceeds of the auction used to convert the hospital structure into apartments for single parents and their children.

Queen of the Most Holy Rosary Parish on Long Island, New York, had a well-established outreach program that offered food, clothing, and financial assistance for rent and other needs. Many who sought help wanted to work, but could not find jobs. Many lacked training and education, and some had been in jail.

With support from Catholic Charities of Rockville Centre, parishioners established a job training and referral service. Volunteers help the unemployed identify training programs and jobs through local papers and other employment services. Parishioners identify jobs in their own companies or odd jobs at home. A parishioner with a background in personnel helps with résumés and interviewing skills. Clients with little work experience are offered volunteer opportunities at the parish. Recently, the local Department of Labor set up an outreach site at the parish.

"We're acting on church teaching about the dignity of work," explains Louise Sandberg, coordinator of outreach for the parish. "We're happy that so many people have gotten jobs."

Advocating for Justice:
Legislative Action

Parishes need to promote a revived sense of political responsibility calling Catholics to be informed and active citizens, participating in the debate over the values and vision that guide our communities and nation. Parishes as local institutions have special opportunities to develop leaders, to promote citizenship, and to provide forums for discussion and action on public issues. Religious leaders need to act in public affairs with a certain modesty, knowing that faith is not a substitute for facts, that values must be applied in real and complex situations, and that people of common faith and good will can disagree on specifics. But parishioners are called to use their talents, the resources of our faith, and the opportunities of this democracy to shape a society more respectful of the life, dignity, and rights of the human person. Parishes can help lift up the moral and human dimension of public issues, calling people to informed participation in the political process.

P arishioners at Corpus Christi Parish in Roseville, Minnesota, are expanding their social ministry to include legislative action. They have set up a parish phone tree with more than thirty members who call or write their elected representative on policy issues affecting children and the poor. As a part of "Voices for Justice," the legislative network of the Archdiocese of St. Paul–Minneapolis, they receive regular "action alerts" on state and federal issues.

At each Mass one recent Sunday, the parish advocacy group spoke in support of a proposal to provide state financing and child care for welfare mothers to complete their education. Postcards were made available in the church vestibule, and over 400 parishioners wrote to their legislators in support of the program.

"We think social justice is an integral part of living our faith," explains parishioner Nonnie Andre. "We need to make the system work for all people. We can't just stand back and say we wish it would work. We need to make it work. We need to be the voices for those who have no voice in legislation decisions."

The voices of parishioners need to be heard on behalf of vulnerable children—born and unborn—on behalf of those who suffer discrimination and injustice, on behalf of those without health care or housing, on behalf of our land and water, our communities and neighborhoods. Parishioners need to bring our values and vision into the debates about a changing world and shifting national priorities. Parishes and parishioners are finding diverse ways to be political without being partisan, joining legislative networks, community organizations, and other advocacy groups. In election years, parishes offer nonpartisan voter registration, education, and forums to involve and inform their members. This kind of genuine political responsibility strengthens local communities as it enriches the witness of our parishes.

Creating Community: Organizing for Justice

Many parishes are joining with other churches and groups to rebuild a sense of community in their own neighborhoods and towns. Parish leaders are taking the time to listen to the concerns of their members and are organizing to act on those concerns. These kind of church-based and community organizations are making a difference on housing, crime, education, and economic issues in local communities. Parish participation in such community efforts develops leaders, provides concrete handles to deal with key issues, and builds the capacity of the parish to act on our values.

The Catholic Campaign for Human Development has provided vital resources to many self-help organizations empowering the poor to seek greater justice. Parish support and participation in these organizations help put Catholic social teaching into action and to revitalize local communities.

In the south Phoenix, Arizona, neighborhood where St. Catherine Parish is located, gangs ruled the streets and drive-by shootings were terrorizing the community. St. Catherine's parishioners decided they had to do something. They contacted an organizer from the Valley Interfaith Project, which is funded by the Catholic Campaign for Human Development, and conducted a six-month series of meetings focused on the problems in the neighborhood and the need for community organization and concern. Parish leaders approached other community leaders and developed a six-point plan with the police and local schools to take back their neighborhood. Street violence was reduced, and the number of parents participating in school events went from twenty to two hundred. Plans are underway with the city of Phoenix to build a multicultural recreation center in the community. And St. Catherine is now working with other churches in Phoenix on wider issues of justice.

At Our Lady of the Miraculous Medal Parish in Los Angeles, California, Catholic Relief Service's Operation Rice Bowl helps parishioners learn about human needs around the globe and offers them an opportunity to act to address those needs. Throughout their Lenten observances—at Masses, in the bulletin, during their Soup Night—information is provided about the international relief programs funded by Operation Rice Bowl (ORB) and the importance of support for this program by U.S. parishes. Families are encouraged to use ORB materials in their own Lenten programs of prayer, fasting, and almsgiving. To supplement the money raised through individual gifts, parishioners sell bread from a local "Justice Bakery." A portion of the proceeds from these sales is kept by the parish and contributed to Operation Rice Bowl programs.

Building Solidarity: Beyond Parish Boundaries

Parishes are called to be communities of solidarity. Catholic social teaching more than anything else insists that we are one family; it calls us to overcome barriers of race, religion, ethnicity, gender, economic status, and nationality. We are one in Christ Jesus (cf. Gal 3:28)—beyond our differences and boundaries.

Parishes need to be bridge-builders, reminding us that we are part of a Universal Church with ties of faith and humanity to sisters and brothers all over the world. Programs of parish twinning, support for Catholic Relief Services, mission efforts, migration and refugee activities, and other global ministries are signs of solidarity in a shrinking and suffering world. Advocacy on human rights, development and peace through legislative networks, and other efforts are also signs of a faith without boundaries and a parish serious about its social responsibilities. A key test of a parish's "Catholicity" is its willingness to go beyond its boundaries to serve those in need and work for global justice and peace. Working with others for common goals across religious, racial, ethnic, and other lines is another sign of solidarity in action.

We hope these seven elements of the social mission of parishes can serve as a framework for planning and assessing parish social ministry. The more practical resources that accompany these reflections may offer some help and assistance in meeting these challenges. National and diocesan structures have materials, resources, and personnel to help parishes assess and strengthen their social ministry.

Lessons Learned

M any parishes have found their community to integrate more fully the social justice dimensions life enriched and strengthened by a serious effort of our faith. They have also learned some lessons.

Rooting Social Ministry in Faith

Parish social action should flow clearly from our faith. It is Jesus who calls us to this task. Social ministry is an expression of who we are and what we believe; it must be anchored in the Scriptures and church teaching. With the eyes of faith, we see every "crack baby" or person with AIDS, every Haitian refugee or Salvadoran immigrant, every victim of unjust discrimination, and every person combatting addiction as a child of God, a sister or brother, as Jesus in disguise. These are not simply social problems, economic troubles, or political issues. They are moral tragedies and religious tests. Parish social ministry is first and foremost a work of faith.

The social mission of the parish begins in the gospel's call to conversion; to change our hearts and our lives; to follow in the path of charity, justice, and peace. The parish is the place we should regularly hear the call to conversion and find help in answering the Lord's call to express our faith in concrete acts of charity and justice.

Respecting Diversity

We are a very diverse community of faith—racially, ethnically, economically, and ideologically. This diversity should be respected, reflected, and celebrated in our social ministry. For example, what works in a predominately African American parish in an urban neighborhood may not be appropriate for a largely white suburban or rural congregation. The issues, approaches, and structures may differ, but our common values unite us. Social justice coalitions across racial, ethnic, and geographic lines can be an impressive sign of the unity of the Body of Christ.

Leadership: Pastors, Councils, Committees, and Educators

While pursuing social justice is a task for every believer, strengthening parish social ministry depends on the skill and commitment of particular parish leaders. Pastors and parish priests have special responsibilities to support integral social ministry. By their preaching, participation, and priorities, they indicate what is important and what is not. They can make it clear that social justice is a mission of the whole parish, not a preoccupation of a few. They are called to teach the authentic social doctrine of the Universal Church.

Other parish staff members and leaders play crucial roles in shaping the quality of parish social ministry. Parish councils in their important planning and advisory functions can help place social ministry in the center parish life. Councils can be a means of collaboration and integration, bringing together liturgy, formation, outreach, and action into a sense of common mission. Councils can play a valuable role in assessing current efforts, setting priorities for the future, and building bridges between parish ministries.

Many parishes have special committees focused on social concerns. These structures can play crucial roles in helping the parish community act on the social justice dimensions of its overall mission. Some parishes have staff members who coordinate social ministry efforts. This is a promising development.

St. Rosa of Lima in Gaithersburg, Maryland, is a parish in a middle-class suburb of Washington, D.C. During the early 1980s, when the federal tax code was overhauled, members of St. Rose proposed sharing their new tax benefit with those in less comfortable circumstances. They set up an annual Social Action Fund drive to which parishioners may contribute their tax savings or any amount they choose. Patterned after the Catholic Campaign for Human Development, the fund provides annual grants to community groups working to change the root causes of neighborhood poverty. Grants totalling over $150,000 have been awarded over the past ten years.

These committees and coordinators best serve parishes by facilitating and enabling the participation of the parish community, rather than simply doing the work on behalf of the parish.

Educators in parish schools, religious education, and formation efforts have special responsibility to share our tradition of social justice as an integral part of our faith. They shape the leaders of the future and by their teaching and example share the social dimensions of our Catholic faith.

Creative and competent leaders—clerical and lay, professional and volunteer—are indispensable for effective parish social ministry. They deserve more assistance, encouragement, financial support, and tools to help them fulfill these demanding roles. Leadership development efforts and ongoing training help parishes strengthen their social ministry capacity.

Links to Diocesan Structures

No parish functions totally by itself. Parish leaders often look to other parishes and diocesan social justice structures for help in fulfilling these responsibilities. Almost all dioceses have social justice structures that offer resources and training for parishes. These structures are diverse including justice and peace commissions, social action offices, CCHD funding and education efforts, rural life offices, and parish social ministry programs of Catholic Charities. Other diocesan groups also offer opportunities for service and action for parishes, for example, Councils of Catholic Women, St. Vincent De Paul Society, Ladies of Charity, ecumenical advocacy and outreach efforts. Many dioceses offer specific "handles" for parish action—legislative networks, work on specific issues or needs, convening parish leaders, providing educational programs coordinating outreach, and so forth. For the most part, parishes cannot go it alone in this area. It is just as clear that diocesan social action can only be effective if it builds parish capacity. Good ties between diocesan and parish efforts are indispensable.

Practicing What We Preach

We also need to try to practice in our own parishes what we preach to others about justice and participation. Too often we are better at talking about justice than demonstrating it, more committed to these values in the abstract than in our everyday ministry. We acknowledge this not to minimize our common efforts, but to acknowledge how far we have yet to go before we fully close the gap between our principles and our performance.

Sensitive, competent, and compassionate pastoral care is an expression of justice. Parish plans and priorities—as well as the use of parish facilities—that reflect the social mission of the Church are expressions of justice. Investing parish resources in social justice and empowering the poor are also expressions of justice. Just personnel policies, fair wages, and equal opportunity efforts are expressions of justice. Respecting and responding to the cultural and ethnic diversity of the communities we serve is an expression of justice. Recognizing the contributions and welcoming the participation of all members of the parish whatever their race, gender, ethnic background, nationality, or disability—these are integral elements of parishes seeking justice.

Some Difficulties and Dangers

In reflecting on the social mission of the parish, the opportunities seem clear. So do some of the difficulties. One danger is the tendency to isolate social ministry, to confine it to the margins of parish life. Another is for social action leaders to isolate themselves, treating the parish as a target rather than a community to be served and empowered.

Another danger is potential partisanship, the temptation to try to use the parish for inappropriate political objectives. We need to make sure our faith shapes our political action, not the other way around. We cannot forget that we pursue the kingdom of God, not some earthly vision or ideological cause.

> *We cannot forget that we pursue the kingdom of God, not some earthly vision or ideological cause.*

A significant challenge is to avoid divisiveness; to emphasize the common ground among social service and social action, education and advocacy, pro-life and social justice, economic development and environmental commitment. We need to work together to reflect a comprehensive concern for the human person in our parish.

Another danger is to try to do too much on too many issues, without clear priorities and an effective plan of action. Not everyone can do everything, but the parish should be a sign of unity in pursuing a consistent concern for human life and human dignity.

The final and most serious danger is for parish leaders to act as if the social ministry of the Church was the responsibility of someone else. Every believer is called to serve those in need, to work for justice, and to pursue peace. Every parish has the mission to help its members act on their faith in the world.

A Final Word of Appreciation, Support, and Challenge

We close these brief reflections with a word of support and encouragement for pastors and parish leaders. The social ministry of the Church is not just another burden, another set of expectations to feel bad about, though in these demanding days it may sometimes seem that way.

The social ministry is already a part of your ministry and leadership. We hope these reflections help you and those you work with to explore how best to carry out this part of your parish's mission. What is strong already? What can be further developed? What needs greater attention? How, given limited time and resources and other obligations, can our parish better share and act on the social justice demands of the gospel?

The Catholic community has been making steady progress in this area. We seek to build on and share these achievements. We know from experience that parishes that strengthen their social ministry enrich every aspect of their parish, bringing increased life and vitality, greater richness, and community to their entire family of faith.

We offer our gratitude and admiration to those who are leading and helping our parishes act on their social mission. We pledge our support to those who pursue this important challenge with new commitment and energy.

In the gospel, we read how John the Baptist's followers came to Jesus and asked, "Are you the one who is to come, or should we look for another?" Jesus responded in this way: "Go and tell John what you hear and see: The blind regain their sight, the lame walk, lepers are cleansed, the deaf hear, the dead are raised, and the poor have the good news proclaimed to them" (Mt 11:3-5).

These are still the signs of Christ among us—parishes across our country who in their own ways are caring for the sick, opening eyes and ears, helping life overcome death, and preaching the good news to the poor.

Today, more than ever, our parishes are called to be communities of "salt" and "light"; to help believers live their faith in their families, communities, work, and world. We need parishes that will not "lose their flavor" nor put their "light under a basket." We seek to build evangelizing communities of faith, justice, and solidarity, where all believers are challenged to bring God's love, justice, and peace to a world in desperate need of the seasoning of the gospel and the light of Catholic teaching.

NOTES
1. U.S. Department of Commerce, Bureau of the Census, 1990.
2. Allan Guttmacher Institute, 1991.
3. UNICEF, *State of the World's Children*, 1992.
4. For a more extensive treatment of Catholic social teaching, see *Excerpts from "Catholic Social Teaching"* (Washington, D.C.: United States Catholic Conference, 2003).

Discussion/Assessment Questions

. . . [W]e believe the Church's social mission is an essential measure of every parish community . . . . We need to build local communities of faith where our social teaching is central, not fringe; where social ministry is integral, not optional; where it is the work of every believer, not just the mission of a few committed people and committees. (Communities of Salt and Light, 6-7)

The following questions are based on the framework for integrating social ministry throughout parish life contained in *Communities of Salt and Light*. They are designed to help pastors, parish councils, staff, committees, and other groups reflect on their parish's social ministry. They provide an opportunity to do a general assessment that can identify both strengths and weaknesses in efforts to integrate the Church's social mission into various aspects of parish ministry. This general assessment can lead to further discussions by those responsible for each area of ministry.

Anchoring Social Ministry: Prayer and Worship

1. In what ways does our parish worship reflect Christ's call to conversion, to service, and to working for justice?

2. During the liturgy, in what ways is the gospel's call to build peace, work for justice, and care for the poor regularly reflected in the general intercessions, in homilies, in our celebrations of special feast days and holidays, and at other appropriate times?

3. How do our sacramental celebrations help us renew our commitment to reconciliation throughout our lives and rededicate ourselves to Jesus' message of love and justice, especially for those in need?

4. What opportunities for prayer, scripture study, and reflection on our Christian vocation does our parish offer? How is our social mission incorporated into these activities?

5. In what ways are our social ministry efforts clearly rooted in Scripture and spirituality, and connected to liturgy and prayer?

Sharing the Message: Preaching and Education

1. How effectively does preaching at our parish reflect the social dimensions of our faith?

2. In what ways is our rich heritage of Catholic social teaching integrated into our school curriculum?

      — our religious education program?
      — our sacramental preparation program?
      — our Christian initiation ministry?
      — our ongoing religious formation and enrichment for adults?

Supporting the "Salt of the Earth": Family, Work, Citizenship

1. Sustaining Christian marriage and shaping family life around gospel values can be difficult in our culture. What concrete and practical support does our parish offer

      — to married couples and to those preparing for marriage (counsel, retreats, small faith communities)?
      — to parents (parenting skills workshops, support groups)?

2. An important opportunity for living our faith is through our work, in everyday decisions and actions, in the way we treat coworkers and customers. How does our parish support our members in practicing Christian values in the workplace?

3. In what ways are parishioners providing leadership in unions, community groups, professional associations, and political organizations? How does our parish support them as they live their faith in these leadership roles?

Serving the "Least of These": Outreach and Charity

1. In what ways is our parish serving those in need?

2. How do parishioners become aware of these opportunities for service and action?

3. How effectively have we involved our parish community in our social ministry efforts?

4. What direction do our service programs provide to our parish efforts in advocacy—in changing the conditions that create poverty and suffering?

Advocating for Justice: Legislative Action

1. How does our parish help parishioners become better informed on public policy issues that impact the poor and vulnerable?

2. In what ways do we encourage our members to become more active citizens, exercising their right to vote and participating in public life?

3. What opportunities does our parish provide for parishioners to speak and act effectively in the public arena on behalf of the poor and vulnerable, to bring our values to debates about local, national, and international policies and priorities?

4. How effectively have we involved our parish community in advocacy efforts?

Creating Community:
Organizing for Justice

1. What community organizations exist in our local community or diocese?

2. How is our parish participating in or supporting such efforts?

Building Solidarity:
Beyond Parish Boundaries

1. In what ways does our parish provide to our members information about the needs of our brothers and sisters, especially the poor and vulnerable, in other lands?

2. What links does our parish have to people, parishes, or other groups around the globe?

3. What opportunities does our parish offer us to act in solidarity on international issues and needs?

Notes